Ducks and Geese

Tessa Potter and Donna Bailey

STECK-VAUGHN
LIBRARY
A Division of Steck-Vaughn Company

These ducks live on a farm.
Some of the ducks lay eggs.
The farmer likes to eat the eggs.

The farmer sells some of the ducks
for their meat.
Some people like to eat duck meat.

Can you see the white duck
with the curly tail?
He is a male.
Male ducks are called drakes.

4

These ducks swim on a pond.
They use their webbed feet
to help themselves swim.

As they swim, the ducks look
for food in the pond.
They like to eat tiny animals and
plants in the water.

6

Sometimes the ducks put their heads
under the water to look for food.
They find tadpoles and
water beetles to eat.

7

Ducks are always hungry.
This farmer gives them grain to eat.

At night the farmer puts the ducks
in a pen.
There they are safe from rats and foxes.

The ducks lay their eggs in nest boxes
inside the pen.

The farmer collects the eggs
every morning.
Then she lets the ducks out of the pen.

One of the ducks has laid four eggs.
The farmer hopes that baby ducks
will grow in these eggs.

Farm ducks are not good mothers.
This duck got off her nest.
Her eggs will get cold.

The farmer puts the eggs
into a hen's nest.
The hen takes care of the eggs.
She sits on them and keeps them warm.

14

After four weeks, the baby ducks
hatch from the eggs.
We call a baby duck a duckling.
The hen takes care of the ducklings
and her chicks, too.

The ducklings are now a day old.
They like to swim on the pond.
They are already good swimmers.
Soon they'll grow into big ducks.

The farmer keeps geese on her farm, too.
The geese make a lot of noise.
A male goose is called a gander.
Can you see the gander in the picture?
He is looking very fierce!

There are many different ducks and geese.

Can you see the geese by this lake?

The geese are much larger than the ducks.

When ducks fly, they go
straight up into the air.
Geese are too big to do that.
They have to run along the ground first.

These snow geese can fly a long way.
Every year they spend the winter
in hot countries.
Then, in the spring, they fly north
to make their nests.

Canada geese also fly well.
These geese are flying north
to find a nesting place.

Canada geese need a lot of space
and water to swim in.
These geese have found a lake with
an island in the middle of it.

The geese make a nest on
the island in the lake.

The goose lays her eggs in the nest.
How many eggs can you see?

When the baby geese hatch, the goose
takes them for a swim.

These are wild ducks.

They are called mallard ducks.

They live on ponds and rivers.

26

The drake mallard has beautiful green feathers on his head.

The female duck is brown.

She sits on her nest by the river.

When the mallard ducks want to find food, they put their tails in the air and their heads under water.

Some ducks dive right under the water to find food.
This tufted duck can stay underwater for nearly one minute.

Can you see the tuft of black feathers
at the back of this drake's head?
That is why he is called a tufted duck.

Ducks and geese often live together.
In this picture you can find ducks,
geese, and swans on the lake.

Index

Reading Consultant: Diana Bentley
Editorial Consultant: Donna Bailey
Supervising Editor: Kathleen Fitzgibbon

Illustrated by Gill Tomblin
Picture research by Suzanne Williams
Designed by Richard Garratt Design

Photographs
Cover: Oxford Scientific Films (Overseas)
Frank Lane Picture Agency: 18 (Roger Wilmshurst) and 19
    (A. Christiansen)
Peter Greenland: 1, 2, 3, 4, 5, 8, 9, 12, 13, 14, 16 and 17
Eric and David Hosking: 22 and 32
NHPA: 15 (E. A. James), 20 (Stephen Krasemann) and 31 (Melvin Grey)
OSF Picture Library: 21 (Barry Walker), 23 and 24 (Breck P. Kent),
    25 (Margot Conte), 26 (Jack Dermid), 27 (Henry R. Fox), 28 (David
    Thompson) and 29 (Dan Suzio)

Library of Congress Cataloging-in-Publication Data: Potter, Tessa. Ducks and geese/Tessa Potter and Donna Bailey;
[illustrated by Gill Tomblin]. p. cm.—(Animal world) SUMMARY: Examines various kinds of ducks and geese, both on the f
and in the wild. ISBN 0-8114-2628-9 1. Ducks—Juvenile literature. 2. Geese—Juvenile literature. [1. Ducks. 2. Geese.]
Bailey, Donna. II. Tomblin, Gill, ill. III. Title. IV. Series: Animal world (Austin, Tex.) SF505.3.P67 1990 598.4′1— dc20
89-22013 CIP AC

2 3 4 5 6 7 8 9 LB 96 95 94 93 92